REAL FAST
WRITING

REAL FAST WRITING

25 of the Hottest, Easy-to-Implement, Under-the-Radar Strategies You Can Use NOW to Write More, Write Better and Write with Panache!

DANIEL HALL

ISBN-13: 978-0-943941-00-4

Printed in the United States of America
Cover and Interior design: 1106 Design

Publisher's Cataloging-In-Publication Data
(Prepared by The Donohue Group, Inc.)

Names: Hall, Daniel, 1965-

Title: Real fast writing : 25 of the hottest, easy-to-implement, under the radar strategies you can use now to write more, write better and write with panache! / by Daniel Hall.

Description: Austin, TX : Real Fast Publications, [2016] | Series: Real fast writing ; [1] | Each method described includes a link to a short online video tutorial.

Identifiers: ISBN 978-0-943941-00-4

Subjects: LCSH: Authorship--Popular works. | English language--Rhetoric--Computer network resources--Popular works.

Classification: LCC PN147 .H35 2016 | DDC 808.02--dc23

To Frustrated Writers. Those of you with the ideas who want to get your message out faster.

CONTENTS

INTRODUCTION

The goal of this book is simple: Help you write faster and at a higher quality.

Let's face it, if you're in business for yourself—a speaker or trainer, coach or consultant—or if you realize the great need for large quantities of fantastic content fast, then you need to know how to speed write.

It goes without saying that, if you're a writer or publisher and you can already crank out content at a brisk clip, even a small increase in production can give you a slight edge. Add a percentage point more production with one tactic here and another percentage point with another strategy there, and if you do that consistently, over time you can significantly increase your overall production.

The fact is this book contains all of the strategies I've learned, developed, or innovated to do exactly that: write at lightning-fast speed.

By the way, the techniques I cover can be applied—almost universally—to any type of content you need. You can use these methods to quickly write books, blog posts, emails, letters, scripts, articles, essays, white papers, sales copy, social media posts, fiction, or non-fiction.

How do I know these strategies will work for you?

Simple. Because they have worked for me!

And God knows if they worked for me, they can most definitely work for YOU. I'm super-confident of that.

You see, I was—and still am—the slowest writer I know.

Gosh . . . I still use the Columbus method of typing. That is, I hunt and land! If you've ever heard me on a webinar typing responses to questions . . . it's painful! So doggone sloooow!

Add to this my years in law school when I was on Law Review, I developed into such an anal-retentive—everything had to be perfect—freak. This experience only slowed me down more.

But when I struck out on my own as a digital publisher, I knew I had to find a way to crank out great content fast when necessary.

Necessity is a mother . . . Ahem, I mean the mother of invention. So, what you have here are those strategies that helped me immensely. And whether you're Sir Speedy or slower than molasses in your writing, there is a technique here to help you write better and faster.

With that said, you're going to get the most out of these strategies if you understand . . .

HOW TO USE
THIS BOOK

THERE ARE 25 DIFFERENT METHODS here that are meant to be consumed as you would a smorgasbord; pick and choose those that best suit you and your needs. They are not necessarily meant to be used all at the same time. I don't think you could even if you wanted to. However, many of the techniques work well in tandem or in groups.

Also, this book is unique in that each method will include a graphic of the tip, a short discussion on how to apply it, AND a short video tutorial.

To watch the video tutorials, simply open a web browser and navigate to—

www.DanielHallPresents.com/rfw

Once there, register for access with your name and email address.

I have endeavored to make these strategies "grab-n-go" easy . . . so, with that brief introduction, let's jump into tip #1 . . .

FAST WRITING TIP #1

Record and Transcribe

WRITE 10 TOPICAL QUESTIONS.
RECORD YOURSELF ANSWERING.
TRANSCRIBE THE RECORDING. EDIT
THE TRANSCRIPTION.
—REALFASTBOOK.COM

HERE'S HOW TO IMPLEMENT IT!

The record-and-transcribe strategy is one of my favorites—probably the reason why it's number one! This strategy is great for people who are good speakers.

The idea is to record a conversation about your topic, and then have the conversation transcribed. Once it's transcribed, you then edit and polish the content into something useable.

FOLLOW THE STEPS

1. It's easier to get great content from this strategy if you start with writing 10 questions about your topic as a guide. These questions can come from frequently asked customer or client questions, or they can come from your experiences. But, as you think of questions, remember that it is easier to go from general to specific in your topic. Also, think about what answers would develop the content you wish to communicate; then ask the questions that would elicit that answer.

2. If possible, have a colleague or friend interview you using the 10 questions as a guide. Encourage your interviewer to ask probing follow-up questions, and tell them to follow up on anything they don't understand.

3. For your part, strive to give the most detailed and thorough answers you can. Be mindful to explain your answers as you would to someone who has no knowledge of your content.

4. Record this interaction as an MP3. I like the free recording software called Audacity if you don't already have a recorder on your machine. (See resources for link.)

5. Have the MP3 transcribed using one of the transcription services. Transcription services are generally reasonably priced. I've listed a few of my favorites in the resources, or you could simply Google "Transcription Services."

6. Finally, edit and polish the transcription. I find that, for me, an hour of conversation yields about 20 typed pages of content. Your yield will depend on how fast (or slow) you speak.

RESOURCES

Audacity Recording Software
http://sourceforge.net/projects/audacity

Fiverr Transcriptionist
http://bit.ly/1IxIHwS

VerbalInk Transcriptions
http://verbalink.com/

Rev Transcriptions
https://www.rev.com/

Note: All Video Tutorials Are Available Here
www.DanielHallPresents.com/rfw

FAST WRITING TIP #2

Use Amazon's "Look Inside" Feature

USE AMAZON'S "LOOK INSIDE" FEATURE TO CREATE FIRST-DRAFT OUTLINE. PERUSE TABLE OF CONTENTS OF RELATED BOOKS. GET INSPIRATION FOR TOPICS AND ORGANIZATION.
—REALFASTBOOK.COM

HERE'S HOW TO IMPLEMENT IT!

I love stuff that allows you to leverage the work of other authors in a legitimate and ethical way. This tip definitely delivers.

The idea is to create a first draft of your contents' outline by using the "Look Inside" feature available on many Amazon book listings. Of course, having an outline increases the speed at which you create content. Much of writing is having a roadmap and knowing where you're going.

However, let me be clear about one thing. I'm not advocating that you plagiarize another author's work. Do not do that. I am saying that you can use this tactic for inspiration and guidance in developing your own outline quickly.

FOLLOW THE STEPS

1. Go to Amazon and search for books on the topic you want to create content on.

2. Using the book's "Look Inside" feature, peruse the Table of Contents.

3. Note how the book is organized and what topics are included.

4. Cherry-pick topics and organization for your own content outline.

5. Oftentimes this is a good starting place to create your 10 questions if you are using Tip #1—Record and Transcribe.

RESOURCES

Amazon
http://amazon.com/

Amazon explains "Look Inside"
http://amzn.to/1KYDca4

Note: All Video Tutorials Are Available Here
www.DanielHallPresents.com/rfw

FAST WRITING TIP #3

Let Nothing Distract You

LET NOTHING DISTRACT. USE A
TIMER. SET FOR 20 MINUTES.
WRITE WITHOUT STOPPING. BREAK
FOR 20 MINUTES. REPEAT.
—REALFASTBOOK.COM

HERE'S HOW TO IMPLEMENT IT!

Good golly, I am so easily distracted.
Squirrel!
See?

Let's face it, if you too are easily distracted I can guarantee that fact will negatively impact your writing productivity. The problem is "focusing" is much easier said than done. At least, that was the deal for me before I used this method to write more in less time. Fortunately, it's a simple fix.

The idea is to use a timer and do nothing but write for short intervals of time. And when I say write, I mean do nothing but write. Not write and edit. Or write and check your email. Write. Period.

Here's the process that works best for me.

FOLLOW THE STEPS

1. Get a timer. A simple egg timer or the timer on your smartphone or a free online timer will do the job fine.

2. Find a conducive environment where you will not be interrupted. If necessary, inform people in your environment that you are not to be disturbed. **Turn off your phone!**

3. Set the timer for 20 minutes. No more. No less.

4. Write without stopping for 20 minutes. If you don't know what to write, write your name over and over. Seriously. After a few minutes of that, you'll start getting ideas quick. Ask me how I know.

5. After 20 minutes of writing, take a break for 20 minutes. Reward yourself. Eat a piece of fruit. Watch your favorite reality TV show. Walk your dog. Do what you like doing.

6. After 20 minutes of break time, repeat the process. You'll be amazed at how much content you can get on a page in a brief time with these short bursts of micro-focused writing.

RESOURCES

Online Timer
http://www.online-stopwatch.com/interval-timer/

Note: All Video Tutorials Are Available Here
www.DanielHallPresents.com/rfw

FAST WRITING TIP #4

Never Write and Edit Simultaneously

2 RULES.
RULE #1 — NEVER WRITE AND EDIT AT THE SAME TIME
RULE #2 — SEE # 1.

— REALFASTBOOK.COM

HERE'S HOW TO IMPLEMENT IT!

If writing and editing at the same time were a crime, they'd lock me up and throw away the key.

The problem with writing and editing at the same time is it's a bit like trying to wash the dishes before finishing your meal. They are independent processes that actually use two different parts of the brain. Unless you are super-human (not likely) you cannot effectively toggle back and forth between them, and trying to will . . . slooooooow . . . you . . . dooown.

The undercurrent of this tip is it mitigates any tendencies to second guess ourselves . . . which takes time to do!

So how do you follow this tip? See below, my edit-happy friend.

FOLLOW THE STEPS

1. Give yourself permission to write less-than-perfect prose. Develop a blind eye to misspellings and punctuation errors, at least on the first draft.

2. If you're tempted to correct and edit as you write, use the editing process as your reward in Fast Writing Tip #3—Let Nothing Distract.

3. Go back and edit only after you've reached a natural stopping place, like the end of a chapter or section. I don't necessarily agree that you have to completely finish writing before moving to editing, because there is something to be said for course corrections that actually improve your writing if you catch problems in time. But again, finish discrete sections of your writing before editing, and you'll get more words on the page faster.

RESOURCES

Note: All Video Tutorials Are Available Here
www.DanielHallPresents.com/rfw

FAST WRITING TIP #5

Set Page Size to Trim Size

TO ENCOURAGE YOU AND SHOW HOW
QUICKLY YOU'RE MAKING PROGRESS,
SET UP YOUR WORD PROCESSOR PAGE
TO THE SAME TRIM SIZE AS YOUR BOOK
(5"X8", 6"X9"). THAT WAY YOU SEE HOW
QUICKLY YOU'RE MAKING PROGRESS
AS YOU WRITE.
—REALFASTBOOK.COM

HERE'S HOW TO IMPLEMENT IT!

Writing, like everything else, gets easier and faster as you build momentum. This tip is all about helping you build momentum in your writing. This strategy is especially useful if you're trying to complete a book. The idea of this tip is to set up your word processing program pages in the same trim size as the book you intend to publish.

The cool thing is that, when you combine this strategy with a 20-minute writing session (a la Tip #3), you see how many approximate pages you've actually written in

YOUR book size . . . It only serves to propel you forward and encourage you to keep going.

It's all about that illusive trip-wire that tells your brain, "Hey, we're making real progress here! Don't stop now."

It's relatively easy to set this up in MS Word. Here's how . . .

FOLLOW THE STEPS

1. Determine the size of the book you want to publish. Find the trim size by searching for similar books to the one you're publishing on Amazon.

Product Details **Equals 5"x8" Trim Size**

Series: Detective Kim Stone crime thriller series
Paperback: 388 pages
Publisher: Bookouture; 1 edition (February 20, 2015)
Language: English
ISBN-10: 190949092X
ISBN-13: 978-1909490925
Product Dimensions: 5.1 x 0.9 x 7.8 inches
Shipping Weight: 13.4 ounces (View shipping rates and policies)
Average Customer Review: ★★★★☆ (549 customer reviews)
Amazon Best Sellers Rank: #9,481 in Books (See Top 100 in Books)

Now, in MS Word, go to "Page Layout" ➟ Size ➟ More Paper Sizes (it's at the bottom of the dialog box) ➟ Page

Setup ➟ Paper ➟ Paper Size ➟ Scroll to bottom and choose "Custom Size" ➟ Type in the inch dimensions of your trim size ➟ Click "OK." Note: I created an animated .gif and included it in the resources below if you want to see this process in action.

2. Start writing directly into the new-sized page.

RESOURCES

Amazon
http://amazon.com/

MS Word Page/ Trim Set Up
http://g.recordit.co/RAGzS1BP7E.gif

Note: All Video Tutorials Are Available Here
www.DanielHallPresents.com/rfw

Nothing but Keyboard Action

CURE FOR WRITER'S BLOCK. DO NOT STOP WRITING FOR 20 MINUTES. EVEN IF IT IS YOUR NAME OR TRANSCRIPTION FROM YOUR FAVORITE MOVIE. NOTHING BUT KEYBOARD ACTION WILL HELP YOU BREAK THROUGH ROUGH PATCHES.
— REALFASTBOOK.COM

HERE'S HOW TO IMPLEMENT IT!

It happens to all of us . . . dreaded WRITER'S BLOCK! This tip, however, will help you break through since it keeps your fingers moving on the keyboard. So even if you can't think of anything to write, you keep typing. Just your name over and over if you have to.

After several minutes of this activity, it is likely that you'll get ideas and you'll start getting them down on the page. That's what counts.

Here's the process . . .

21

FOLLOW THE STEPS

1. If you have writer's block, your first step is to let it go. Relax. Often our anxiety about our writer's block keeps us stuck. So just let go of the outcome.

2. Now, sit at your keyboard and start typing your name, or your favorite quote, or the "Lord's Prayer." It actually doesn't matter what you're typing as long as your fingers are flying across the keyboard and words are appearing on the screen. There is something about this otherwise mindless psychomotor activity that resets the brain and gets the juices (and ideas) flowing again.

RESOURCES

Note: All Video Tutorials Are Available Here
www.DanielHallPresents.com/rfw

FAST WRITING TIP #7

Don't Write, Present

PREPARE A SLIDE PRESENTATION OF EACH
CHAPTER OF YOUR BOOK USING IMAGES AND
BULLET POINTS. NOW TEACH YOUR PRESEN-
TATIONS AS YOU RECORD AND TRANSCRIBE
THEM. YOU'LL HAVE LOTS OF PROSE. FAST.
—REALFASTBOOK.COM

HERE'S HOW TO IMPLEMENT IT!

If you like to teach, you're going to love this strategy.
This method is a cool variation of Tip #1—Record and
Transcribe.

That is, instead of writing your book, you pretend to
present the content as if you were doing it at a seminar.
You record your "presentation" and transcribe it.

If you find it easier to write bullet points on a slide presentation than you do to write fully developed sentences
on a word processor, this is the strategy for you.

Just follow this process and you'll see how easy it is to crank out grade-A great content fast.

FOLLOW THE STEPS

1. Organize your key points onto slides. Many times I will organize my content by using a combination of Tip #2—Use Amazon's "Look Inside"—my own knowledge base, and PowerPoint slides. Organize the content as you would if you were going to deliver the "lecture" as an assignment in college.

2. Then turn on your recorder and teach your slide presentation. It's important to use your bullet points to riff-off on. They are intended to remind you of what you should be teaching. Often I find it's easier if I approach it as though I were explaining each point. Keep in mind that it is impossible to be too detailed.

3. Transcribe, edit, and polish as in Tip #1.

RESOURCES

Google's Free Slide Presentation Software
https://www.google.com/slides/about/

Note: All Video Tutorials Are Available Here
www.DanielHallPresents.com/rfw

Letter (or Email) to a Friend

WRITE TO A FRIEND. IT'S MUCH EASIER TO WRITE TO A SPECIFIC PERSON THAN IT IS TO WRITE TO A NEBULOUS AUDIENCE. SO COMMUNICATE THE CONTENT OF YOUR BOOK IN A LONG "LETTER" TO A FRIEND KEEPING A SPECIFIC PERSON IN MIND AS YOU WRITE.
—REALFASTBOOK.COM

HERE'S HOW TO IMPLEMENT IT!

This is another one of those mind hacks that takes the pressure off you. All you have to do is have a (written) conversation with a friend, something you probably do all of the time.

The idea of this tip is to write the content of your book in the form of a letter or email to your best friend. This works well for a couple of different reasons.

First, you will have someone specifically in mind as you explain your content; therefore, your explanations will be more thorough and complete. Further, psychologically you'll have a vested interest in making sure that your friend "gets it." Additionally, it's just more difficult to write to some vague, unknown audience. When you have just one person in mind, you'll also have a better idea of how to approach the content for that particular person, but chances are that the explanations you provide to that one person will be understandable to most other readers as well. Last, and perhaps most important, you know that your best friend probably won't judge your writing too harshly.

Here's the process to make it happen.

FOLLOW THE STEPS

1. Start each letter or email as you would any other. Dear Sally . . ..

2. Write to your best friend and explain your content. As long as your friend doesn't mind (and even if they do), actually send the letter to them.

3. Make each chapter or sub-chapter its own letter.

4. Repeat until your content is out of your head and on the page.

RESOURCES

Note: All Video Tutorials Are Available Here
www.DanielHallPresents.com/rfw

FAST WRITING TIP #9

Start with a Quote

IT'S OFTEN EASIER TO START WRITING
WHEN THERE ARE ALREADY WORDS
ON THE PAGE. SO FIND CONTENT-
RELATED QUOTES AND USE THEM
AS A SPRINGBOARD TO JUMP START
YOUR WRITING.
—REALFASTBOOK.COM

"The last thing we discover in composing a work is what to put down first."

—BLAISE PASCAL, THE MIND ON FIRE:
A FAITH FOR THE SKEPTICAL AND INDIFFERENT

HERE'S HOW TO IMPLEMENT IT!

Sometimes it's difficult to get started when you're staring at a blank computer screen and watching that blasted blinking cursor.

The idea behind this little hack is to start each chapter or sub-chapter with a relevant quote. Often, when something already exists on the page, it is easier to write. The quote can also give you tone and direction. It can jump-start your juices and get the ideas flowing. Even if that means explaining how the quote pertains to your content.

Here's the process I use when I'm using quotes as a writing springboard.

FOLLOW THE STEPS

1. As long as you know what content you want to cover in your writing, start off by finding a relevant quote.

2. Do a Google search for quotes related to your topic, even if that is "Gardening Quotes" or "Police Quotes." I've included a great list of quote sites in the resources below.

3. I choose quotes based on how they "pop" off the page and whether they immediately inspire ideas in me.

4. Once you've chosen your quote, get it on the page, and start writing. If you have to explain how the quote is relevant to your content to get started, do it.

RESOURCES

A Great List of Quote Sites
http://list.ly/list/1dS-best-quote-sites

Note: All Video Tutorials Are Available Here
www.DanielHallPresents.com/rfw

Here are the runner-up quotes that did not make the top of this tip, but I thought you'd enjoy nonetheless.

"Who is more to be pitied, a writer bound and gagged by policemen or one living in perfect freedom who has nothing more to say?"

—Kurt Vonnegut

"Biting my truant pen, beating myself for spite: 'Fool!' said my muse to me, 'look in thy heart, and write.'"

—Philip Sidney, Astrophel and Stella

FAST WRITING TIP #10

Start with an Image

OFTEN IT'S EASIER TO START YOUR WRITING BY DESCRIBING A CONTENT-RELATED IMAGE. START EACH NEW SECTION OF YOUR BOOK WITH AN IMAGE; THEN DESCRIBE THE IMAGE IN THE CONTEXT OF YOUR CONTENT.
—REALFASTBOOK.COM

HERE'S HOW TO IMPLEMENT IT!

This tip makes it super-easy to write. The adage "a picture is worth a thousand words" is accurate, but what many writers miss is the fact that they can take the words that the image evokes and get them on the page.

In fact, in most instances I would argue that an image is worth a great many more than 1,000 words.

That is the thrust of this strategy, which, like Tip #9—Start with a Quote, is intended to jump-start your writing by simply describing what the image means within the context of the content of your work.

Easy-peasy, right? Here are the steps to make it happen . . .

FOLLOW THE STEPS

1. Look at your outline, and choose images that correspond to the content of your chapters and sub-chapters.

2. Like quotes, they should be chosen not only on the basis of being relevant to your specific content, but also to the ideas the image evokes in you.

3. Include an image at the beginning of each section, chapter, or sub-chapter of your book.

4. You can also include a quote if you'd like. However, whatever you decide to do, be consistent. That is, if you start with an image and a quote, carry that through to each chapter.

5. Make sure that the images are royalty free and/or public domain. Do not use copyrighted or trademarked images without permission. I have included a list of some of my favorite image sites below.

RESOURCES

Pixabay (Free)
http://pixabay.com/

Freeimages (Free)
http://www.freeimages.com/

Big Stock Photo (Paid)
http://powerpointpix.com

Iconfinder (Free & Paid)
https://www.iconfinder.com/

Note: All Video Tutorials Are Available Here
www.DanielHallPresents.com/rfw

FAST WRITING TIP #11

Mind Map Hack

MIND MAP YOUR OUTLINE. DOWNLOAD
AND INSTALL FREEMIND SOFT-
WARE. GOOGLE IT; IT'S FREE. USE
FREE ASSOCIATION TO FLESH OUT
TOPIC. ORGANIZE INTO A DETAILED
WRITING OUTLINE.
— REALFASTBOOK.COM

HERE'S HOW TO IMPLEMENT IT!

Mind maps are a great way to brainstorm and organize content quickly. It is very easy to mind map your outlines.

So what are mind maps? According to Wikipedia, "A mind map is a diagram used to visually organize information. A mind map is often created around a single concept, drawn as an image in the center of a blank landscape page, to which associated representations of ideas such as images, words and parts of words are added."

I like to think of mind maps as wagon wheels where, at the hub, you start with your main idea. Then you connect spokes (or child branches) of related topics. And then you add child branches to your child branches, and so on.

Mind maps work particularly well for non-linear thinkers (like me). I like them best because they accommodate and help to organize ideas and topics that are in no particular order. The visual nature of mind maps helps you to see connections and organize those topics and ideas in a logical way.

Perhaps the most important benefit of working from a mind map is that it sparks new and related ideas, and it encourages you to add new child branches.

Here's the process to make your first mind map.

FOLLOW THE STEPS

1. Download Freemind (Free mind map software).

2. Complete your mind map.

3. Use the mind map to do a detailed outline.

4. Start writing by following the outline.

RESOURCES

Download Freemind (Free)
http://freemind.sourceforge.net/wiki/index.php/
Download

Excellent Free Training on Using Freemind
http://bit.ly/1Iv37br

Note: All Video Tutorials Are Available Here
www.DanielHallPresents.com/rfw

Become Perfectly Imperfect

AS AN AUTHOR YOUR JOB IS TO
WRITE (AS MUCH AS POSSIBLE).
TURN OVER RESPONSIBILITY TO
POLISHING AND PERFECTING TO
AN EDITOR.
—REALFASTBOOK.COM

HERE'S HOW TO IMPLEMENT IT!

I'll start by saying that perfection is the enemy of completion. Be that as it may, I am immensely grateful for my legal education and the time I spent as a Law Review editor. Law school taught me precision and accuracy with every word I wrote or spoke. In effect, law school encouraged and even demanded **perfection** especially if the words were written.

That is to say my experiences in law school fueled my pre-existing perfection proclivities (not to mention alliteration ;-)). Now, as a lawyer, these tendencies are not altogether bad. We want precision in law. But as a content provider, running a business in the real world, perfectionism can sink you and drastically reduce your production.

When I struck out on my own as a digital publisher, I quickly realized that, to be as productive as I needed to be, I had to give up on perfection. So do you. Calling something done is vastly better than calling it perfect. What this effectively means is you must concentrate on content *production* and leave the editing and polishing to other people.

Notice I did not say, "Give up on quality." That needs to be great. Nonetheless, if you get your best content out and then let others edit and polish it, you'll be far more productive AND have good quality material.

Here's how to make this tip work:

FOLLOW THE STEPS

1. Realize that perfectionism slows you down and costs you money.

2. Concentrate on writing content that people want to consume. Alas, your job as a content creator is to create content.

3. Hire editors to edit and polish your stuff. A list of outsourcers is included below.

4. Remember, done is better than perfect.

RESOURCES

Fiverr
http://bit.ly/1KYFcis

Craigslist
http://www.craigslist.org/about/sites

Upwork
http://bit.ly/1J7ErF1

Note: All Video Tutorials Are Available Here
www.DanielHallPresents.com/rfw

Let Google Suggest

USE GOOGLE SUGGEST TO DEVELOP
A DETAILED OUTLINE. AS YOU TYPE
YOUR KEYWORDS INTO GOOGLE,
PAY ATTENTION TO WHAT IT
"SUGGESTS." USE TO DEVELOP A
DETAILED OUTLINE.
—*REALFASTBOOK.COM*

HERE'S HOW TO IMPLEMENT IT!

I'm all about harnessing technology to do some of the content creation heavy lifting; Google will help you for free.

It's called "Google Suggest," and you've probably seen it thousands of times but did not realize you could use it to help create content. Google Suggest is the feature that suggests other searches as you enter your keywords into Google. The idea is to pay attention and cherry-pick related topics to include in your outline or mind map.

Here's how . . .

FOLLOW THE STEPS

1. Type your main topic into Google.

2. Drill down as you find relevant and interesting topics.

3. Add new topics to your outline as you deem appropriate.

4. **Bonus:** Try Ubersuggest to turbo-charge your "Google Suggest" searches.

RESOURCES

Google
http://google.com

Ubersuggest
http://ubersuggest.org/

Note: All Video Tutorials Are Available Here
www.DanielHallPresents.com/rfw

FAST WRITING TIP #14

Borrow Expertise

INTERVIEW AN EXPERT. ASK PROB-
ING QUESTIONS. RECORD AND
TRANSCRIBE CONVERSATION.
USE AS A STARTING PLACE FOR
YOUR WRITING.
—*REALFASTBOOK.COM*

HERE'S HOW TO IMPLEMENT IT!

You can add so much more depth and value to your writing if you simply interview experts in the field of your subject.

Let's face it; no matter how much of an expert you are, you can always increase the value of your content by getting other experts to weigh in.

And they will.

All you have to do is ask. Many times I will offer to give them a little promotion as well. By the way, this technique is great for building new and helpful relationships and possibly joint ventures.

Here's how to do it . . .

FOLLOW THE STEPS

1. Choose experts in your field you would like to interview for your project.

2. Email them and explain that you appreciate their work and would like to interview and perhaps feature them in your book or content. Let them know that you would be happy to include their website or other promotional information.

3. Schedule a conference call or Google Hangout and do the interview. Make sure you record and then have your interview transcribed.

4. Include relevant material in your book.

5. **Bonus:** Use news reporter services to find experts. Placing an ad in the services below is free and will likely connect you with experts you never knew about.

RESOURCES

Google Hangouts On-Air
*http://www.google.com/+/learnmore/hangouts/onair.
html*

Free Conference Call
https://www.freeconferencecall.com/

Help a Reporter
http://www.helpareporter.com/

Pitchrate
http://pitchrate.com/

Note: All Video Tutorials Are Available Here
www.DanielHallPresents.com/rfw

Make Writing a Habit

WRITE AT LEAST 500 WORDS PER
DAY (WITHOUT FAIL). IT CONDI-
TIONS YOU TO AUTOMATICALLY
AND EFFORTLESSLY CRANK OUT
PROSE DAILY.
—REALFASTBOOK.COM

"Discipline allows magic. To be a writer is to be the very best of assassins. You do not sit down and write every day to force the Muse to show up. You get into the habit of writing every day so that when she shows up, you have the maximum chance of catching her, bashing her on the head, and squeezing every last drop out of that bitch."

—LILI ST. CROW

HERE'S HOW TO IMPLEMENT IT!

You've heard the saying "The more you do it, the easier it gets."

So, too, with writing.

Even when you're not working on a writing project, write. This is to say you should always have a writing project cooking.

Habit is a very powerful force indeed, and harnessing it to write will yield very good results. Here's the process to make it happen.

FOLLOW THE STEPS

1. Put writing on your calendar. Choose the best time of day or night. For example, I like to write early in the morning, when there are no distractions.

2. Get support from family members. Tell them you're trying to establish a writing habit, and enlist their help.

3. Do not get up from the keyboard until you have cranked out at least 500 words . . . to start.

4. Write in short, 20-minute bursts as discussed in Fast Writing Tip #3—Let Nothing Distract.

RESOURCES

Google Calendar
https://www.google.com/calendar

Note: All Video Tutorials Are Available Here
www.DanielHallPresents.com/rfw

Order Chicken Soup

GO CHICKEN SOUP. COLLECT
STORIES AND OTHER CONTENT
FROM OTHERS. USE TO CREATE
ANTHOLOGIES AND COMPILATIONS.
ADD YOUR OWN CONTRIBUTIONS.
—*REALFASTBOOK.COM*

HERE'S HOW TO IMPLEMENT IT!

Anthologies are a way to put together a book relatively fast.

Here's the idea of this strategy. You collect anecdotes, stories, and/or tips around a common theme from a variety of experts, add your own, and compile the collection into a book.

Here's how to make it happen . . .

FOLLOW THE STEPS

1. Decide on the theme of your book.

2. Determine what contributors get. If it is a business book, offering free inclusion and promotion in the book is enough.

3. Invite contributors.

4. Communicate writing requirements, including deadlines.

5. Collect, compile, and edit material. Use Basecamp or Google Docs for project management.

6. Publish the book.

7. Elicit marketing help from contributors.

RESOURCES

Basecamp
https://basecamp.com/

Google Docs
https://www.google.com/docs/about/

Note: All Video Tutorials Are Available Here
www.DanielHallPresents.com/rfw

Just Have a Convo

HAVE A CONVERSATION ABOUT YOUR TOPIC ON A CONFERENCE LINE. KEEP IT FREE FLOWING BUT LOGICAL. RECORD, TRANSCRIBE, EDIT OUT BEST STUFF.
— REALFASTBOOK.COM

HERE'S HOW TO IMPLEMENT IT!

This is another variation of the Record and Transcribe strategy that we covered in Tip #1. What's different about it is that it is much less structured and therefore easier.

The idea is to jump on a conference call or do an in-person conversation with a friend, colleague, or family member who is also knowl-edgeable about the subject matter, and just have a conversation about the topic and record it. Then transcribe and use the good stuff you say.

Obviously, this is a much freer form than writing out questions or teaching from a PowerPoint or outline that you took the time to create. Consequently, you may yield less usable content than if you took a more organized approach.

Regardless, if you follow the process below, I can almost guarantee that you'll get lots of great-quality content for your writing project.

FOLLOW THE STEPS

1. Start by agreeing on the theme of the conversation. In other words, decide what you are going to talk about.

2. Coach your convo partner to follow up on anything they don't understand, and ask probing questions.

3. Record it.

4. Transcribe, edit, and polish the best stuff as in Tip #1.

RESOURCES

Audacity Recording Software
http://sourceforge.net/projects/audacity

Fiverr Transcriptionist
http://bit.ly/1IxIHwS

VerbalInk Transcriptions
http://verbalink.com/

Note: All Video Tutorials Are Available Here
www.DanielHallPresents.com/rfw

Blog a Book

WRITE AT LEAST ONE 500+ WORD POST RELATED TO THE TOPIC EVERY DAY. IN 30 DAYS, YOU'LL HAVE ENOUGH FOR A 15K-WORD BOOK. —*REALFASTBOOK.COM*

HERE'S HOW TO IMPLEMENT IT!

So much of writing production is a head game. But like any other big project, you eat the elephant one bite at a time. One way to tackle a large (or small) writing project without it seeming overwhelming is to blog a book.

The idea behind this method is to simply write one 500-word blog post every day related to the topic of your book for 30 days. That will yield a nice and manageable 15k-word manuscript perfect for publishing as a Kindle or Print on Demand book.

Here's how to do it . . .

FOLLOW THE STEPS

1. Develop a general outline of the posts you will do (refer to Tips #2—Use Amazon's "Look Inside" and Tip #10—Mind Map and Tip #13—Use Google "Suggest" in developing a robust outline).

2. If you don't already have one, start a blog (see Resources below for free alternatives).

3. Write at least one 500-word post following your outline. What you'll find is that some days the words will flow easier than others. On those days, don't limit yourself to 500 words; if you're on a roll, keep going.

4. Allow yourself to edit and polish every day AFTER the post is completed.

5. Keep this schedule for at least 30 days.

6. Compile all your posts into a manuscript.

RESOURCES

Blogger
http://blogger.com/

WordPress
https://signup.wordpress.com/signup/

Note: All Video Tutorials Are Available Here
www.DanielHallPresents.com/rfw

FAQ Gold

ANSWER CUSTOMER QUESTIONS.
EVERY CUSTOMER QUESTION IS
A POTENTIAL NEW CHAPTER OR
SUB-CHAPTER. ANSWER EACH
QUESTION THOROUGHLY. COMPILE
RESPONSES INTO YOUR BOOK.
—*REALFASTBOOK.COM*

HERE'S HOW TO IMPLEMENT IT!

If you're writing about a topic related to your business, one of the richest sources of content direction is your customers.

The idea behind this tip is this: You are probably already very adept at answering your customers' questions; you simply take the time to reduce these answers to writing. Essentially, you create a super-FAQ (Frequently Asked Questions).

While you may not have enough content for an entire book, I can guarantee that you'll have enough for at least one chapter.

Here's the process . . .

FOLLOW THE STEPS

1. Compile a list of questions you've received from your customers. Check email support, your business's Facebook page, or any other channel you use for customer support.

2. You can beef up the question list by asking your customers what questions they have.

3. Thoroughly answer those questions in written format.

4. Consider using Tip #1—Record and Transcribe—to make the process faster (see Resource example).

5. Compile all your responses into a chapter or short book.

RESOURCES

Amazon Book Example
http://amzn.to/1GZYj7Z

Note: All Video Tutorials Are Available Here
www.DanielHallPresents.com/rfw

Make Downtime Uptime

WRITE WHILE YOU WAIT. REGARD
YOUR SMARTPHONE OR TABLET AS
WRITING TOOLS. WRITE ANYTIME
YOU HAVE DOWNTIME
—*REALFASTBOOK.COM*

HERE'S HOW TO IMPLEMENT IT!

You're going to love this tip! Because today's smartphones and tablets are essentially powerful and portable computers, you can use any downtime or wait time to write.

Waiting in your dentist's office? Write! Waiting for your child after school? Write! Anytime you find yourself waiting—you write!

You'll be amazed at how much you accomplish when you have a productive strategy for all those inevitable wait times.

Here's how to make the most of them . . .

FOLLOW THE STEPS

1. Choose a word processing program for your device. If
   you're on iPhone or iPad, I really like the Pages app (it's
   $9.99). If you're on Android, check out Google Docs
   (it's free), which is fully integrated with Google Drive.
   Now familiarize yourself with the app.

2. Always carry your device.

3. Stay alert to opportunities. Waiting is such a routine
   part of most lives that often we don't realize we're
   waiting. Tune in.

4. Keep your writing project in Google Drive or iCloud so
   you have access to it regardless of the device you're on.

5. Consider dictating into your device for faster production.

6. Get more done in less time by converting downtime
   into uptime.

RESOURCES

Pages for iOS
https://www.apple.com/ios/pages/

Google Docs
https://www.google.com/docs/about/

Dictating With Pages
https://youtu.be/7SU8uPJHqVs

Note: All Video Tutorials Are Available Here
www.DanielHallPresents.com/rfw

Play More

PLAY! BREAK THROUGH WRITERS BLOCK BY TAKING PLAY SESSIONS WHILE YOU WRITE.
—REALFASTBOOK.COM

HERE'S HOW TO IMPLEMENT IT!

OK, throughout this entire book, I've been sharing ways to work more effectively. On the other hand, surprisingly, you may be able to write more and write at a higher quality if you make more time to PLAY.

It seems like the brain works more effectively when you engage in play, especially if you're experiencing writer's block. Fortunately, one of the best techniques to form the habit of creative writing is to reward yourself with play.

Here's how to play more and write more.

FOLLOW THE STEPS

1. Plan how you'll play.

2. If you're using Tip #3—Let Nothing Distract—and working in 20-minute work-rest intervals, make your playtime a reward for a well-written 20-minute writing romp. Because of endorphin release during your rewards, it'll quickly become easier and easier to write.

3. As you play, totally let go of your writing project and just take a mini-mental vacation from it.

4. When you go back to work, words will flow more effortlessly, and your writing is likely to be of a higher caliber.

RESOURCES

Recommended reading—Flow
http://amzn.to/1Iv6wXG

Note: All Video Tutorials Are Available Here
www.DanielHallPresents.com/rfw

Quiet Your Mind

CLOSE YOUR EYES. CONCENTRATE
ON YOUR BREATH FOR 10 MINUTES.
BE OPEN TO THE IDEAS AS THEY
COME. WRITE THEM DOWN.
—REALFASTBOOK.COM

HERE'S HOW TO IMPLEMENT IT!

The voices—the self-talk—all that noise going on between your ears. It's no wonder you have trouble focusing enough to write.

The solution? Quiet your mind before you start to write.

Easier said than done in our hectic lives, but try the process below, and practice it before each writing session. My bet is that, over time, not only will it benefit your writing but other parts of your life as well.

FOLLOW THE STEPS

1. Quieting your mind is all about relaxation and breathing.

2. Sit in a comfortable position.

3. Become aware of your body. Relax from out to in. Close your eyes and start with your fingers and toes, and slowly relax toward your core.

4. Now start focusing on your breathing. All of your attention should be put on breathing out and in.

5. When you notice that your mind starts to wander to other things, bring your attention back to your breathing. Continue to monitor your relaxation.

6. Do this for 10 minutes before each writing session, and then be open to any of the ideas that pop into your brain.

RESOURCES

Note: All Video Tutorials Are Available Here
www.DanielHallPresents.com/rfw

FAST WRITING TIP #23

Account for Yourself

GET AN ACCOUNTABILITY PARTNER.
AGREE WITH ANOTHER WRITER/
AUTHOR. REPORT TO EACH OTHER
AT LEAST ONCE A WEEK.
—REALFASTBOOK.COM

HERE'S HOW TO IMPLEMENT IT!

It's true; you'll definitely get more done when you have to answer to someone else. However, most of our writing projects we do for ourselves and, accordingly, we only have to answer to ourselves. This can be a problem because we are rarely as disciplined when we answer to no one.

The idea behind this strategy is to find an accountability partner to hold each other accountable and on track.

Here's how to set it up . . .

FOLLOW THE STEPS

1. Find a writer or author who also wants to get more done by having an accountability partner. You can find this person among your present contacts, or you can join a writers' group and find a partner there.

2. Meet and establish criteria. What will your meeting schedule be? This should be at least weekly. What are the consequences if you fail to meet a goal?

3. Make realistic accountability goals. Remember, even small movements forward can yield big results over time.

4. Start meeting and moving forward.

5. Consider also using an online service where you have skin in the game (money) and the consequence of not reaching your goal is you lose money. Check out the resources below.

RESOURCES

21 Habit—Invest In Yourself
http://www.21habit.com/

Go F*ck*ng Do It
https://gofuckingdoit.com/

Note: All Video Tutorials Are Available Here
www.DanielHallPresents.com/rfw

Visual Reminders

WRITE AND POST YOUR WRITING
GOALS. STICK THEM IN YOUR WORK
SPACE, ON THE FRIDGE AND BATH-
ROOM MIRROR. THEY ARE CON-
STANT REMINDERS TO WRITE.
—*REALFASTBOOK.COM*

HERE'S HOW TO IMPLEMENT IT!

This strategy is super easy to implement and is quite effective. You leave visual reminders for yourself of your writing goal.

The idea behind this tip is, if you're off track and are reminded of your goal, it is more likely that you'll get back on target.

Here's what to do . . .

FOLLOW THE STEPS

1. Determine your writing goal. Suggestion: At least 500 words a day.

2. Write Post-its with your goal, and post near your computer and in your writing space.

3. Also, post your writing goal on your calendar. I use my Google calendar to do this.

4. Read your goal often but at least twice daily.

RESOURCES

Google Calendar
https://www.google.com/calendar

Note: All Video Tutorials Are Available Here
www.DanielHallPresents.com/rfw

A Tip a Day

WRITE A TIP A DAY. AFTER YOU'VE COLLECTED 25 TIPS GO BACK AND EXPLAIN EACH TIP. THEN COMPILE INTO A BOOK ;-)
—REALFASTBOOK.COM

HERE'S HOW TO IMPLEMENT IT!

I will admit that this very book was written using this technique, so you obviously know it works.

The idea behind this tip is breaking your project up into easily achievable daily goals. That means it should be no problem for you to write a tip or two every single day. Once you have them, simply explain them.

Here's how to do it . . .

FOLLOW THE STEPS

1. Write out at least one tip a day related to your business or core expertise.

2. Organize tips into a logical order.

3. I like to leverage my tips by simultaneously making graphics out of them. I use a $2.99 app for my iPhone called WordSwag. All of the tip graphics in this book were initially made with WordSwag. But you can also use Canva online, which is free.

4. Once you have your tips, go back and explain and develop each one so that they are easily consumable.

5. Explain all the tips and, *voila*, you have a manuscript with super-helpful tips for your target audience.

RESOURCES

Canva
https://www.canva.com/

Word Swag
http://wordswag.co/

Note: All Video Tutorials Are Available Here
www.DanielHallPresents.com/rfw

Repackage and Repurpose (Bonus)

REPACKAGE AND REPURPOSE EARLIER WORK. USE IN PART OR WHOLE IN YOUR NEW WORK.
—REALFASTBOOK.COM

HERE'S HOW TO IMPLEMENT IT!

I love to leverage assets, intellectual and otherwise. The fact is this book came into being because I realized I had these fast-writing graphics. So, why not use them to write this book?

The story is I created these graphics for a course my friend John Kremer and I did called Real Fast Social Graphics (formerly Real Fast Pinterest). These graphics were posted on Pinterest to promote another one of my training products called Real Fast Book.

The lesson: I used the same content (the fast-writing tips) to prove the concept of Real Fast Social Graphics, to drive traffic to my opt-in page for Real Fast Book and as a basis for this book, *Real Fast Writing.* Continuing in the same vein, I wrote this book so I could illustrate how to use Amazon's Textbook Creator software and create a product for that.

Now that's leverage!

And you can do the same with your past work. Here's how . . .

FOLLOW THE STEPS

1. Take stock of what you've got. This means compiling all completed material in one file folder for easy access.

2. With every new writing project, consider where and how you might re-use something you already have.

3. The reverse idea is also valid. That is, if you're writing something completely original now, be mindful of how you may use it in the future. It's what this book is about. Namely, I knew that I'd use it in the future as part of a product for the Kindle Textbook Creator. It's all about leverage.

RESOURCES

Note: All Video Tutorials Are Available Here
www.DanielHallPresents.com/rfw

If you're interested in creating Kindle books
that contain audio and video, check out my
course on using the Kindle Textbook Creator at
http://kindlepublishersuperpack.com

Start With Public Domain (Bonus)

KICKSTART YOUR NEW WORK WITH PUBLIC-DOMAIN CONTENT. ADD YOUR OWN INSIGHTS AND VALUE. FRESHEN UP THE CONTENT AS NEEDED. GET WAY AHEAD OF THE WRITING CURVE.
—*REALFASTBOOK.COM*

HERE'S HOW TO IMPLEMENT IT!

I am proud to say that I have made thousands of dollars in my business publishing public-domain work or work derived from the public domain. In fact, it is such a cornerstone to my publishing business that I have collaborated on several public-domain online educational courses dealing with using this type of content in books, online courses, blog posts, videos, audio books, Kindle and Barnes & Noble eBooks. Which is to illustrate that public domain can be used practically anywhere.

And your first question might be: what is public domain?

According to the Public Domain Sherpa website, "**the public domain consists of works that aren't protected by copyright** or by other legal means. You are free to use public domain works however you wish, without seeking permission, because . . .

- their copyrights have expired; or

- the copyright owner didn't follow certain required formalities (so they didn't get a valid copyright); or

- the works weren't eligible for copyright in the first place; or

- their creators dedicated them to the public domain."

Consequently, you can use public-domain content to riff-off on, add value to, and produce derivative works.

This is much akin to **Tip #9 Start with a Quote** and **Tip #10 Start with an Image.** That is, you're using content already in existence and adding to it. Of course, like Tips 9 and 10, you can use your public-domain content anywhere in your writing project where it makes sense.

One other point I want to make about using public domain is, when many people hear "public domain" they think old, stale content and therefore not good to use.

Please allow me to dispel this thought. While it is true there is much older public-domain content; just because it is old doesn't make it un-useable. For example, how many different ways are there to grow tomato plants? Or do calisthenics? Or pitch a tent? In other words, older public-domain content works great for evergreen topics.

Further, there is much current, cutting-edge content that is released into the public domain. For example, many people are unaware that almost everything that the United States federal government produces goes into the public domain automatically. And, keep in mind, that the U.S. government is the single largest content creator in the world!

It's all there and freely available for your use! (Check the resources below.)

Here's how to use public domain in your projects . . .

FOLLOW THE STEPS

1. Find appropriate public-domain content. I've listed some of my favorite resources below.

2. Insure the content that you want to use is actually in the public domain. Do this by checking the license on the site where you obtain the material. It should clearly indicate that the material is in the public domain or be marked Creative Commons, public domain.

3. Here's an example of one such license from Project Gutenberg:

> **Our ebooks may be freely used in the United States** because most are not protected by U.S. copyright law, usually because their copyrights have expired. They may not be free of copyright in other countries. Readers outside of the United States must check the copyright laws of their countries before downloading or redistributing our ebooks. We also have a number of copyrighted titles, for which the copyright holder has given permission for unlimited non-commercial worldwide use.

4. Now add your own spin to the content, making sure to add value and context. The reasons for the use of the content should be clear and should move the reader further along or in some way help them.

RESOURCES

Project Gutenberg
https://www.gutenberg.org/

USA.gov
https://www.usa.gov/

Hathi Trust Digital Library
https://www.hathitrust.org/

Comic Book +
http://comicbookplus.com/

Internet Archive
https://archive.org/

Library of Congress
https://www.loc.gov/

U.S. Government Printing Office
https://www.loc.gov/

Google Books
https://books.google.com/

FURTHER READING

Public Domain Sherpa
http://publicdomainsherpa.com/

Real Fast Public Domain (my online course)
http://realfastpublicdomain.com/

Real Fast Derivative Product
http://realfastderivativeproducts.com/

A FOND FAREWELL

You've got good things to say, good things to write. I know the tips in this book will help you say them and write them faster.

So pick the strategy that you like the best. Master it. Add another complementary strategy, or not. It's up to you.

For as long as you keep writing and completing your writing projects, this book will have done its job. And I would love to hear about your experiences with these tips. Please share them with me in my Facebook group. Ask to join here—*https://www.facebook.com/groups/danielhall/*

Also, if you're ready to publish your book, you may want to check out the free step-by-step training I have for you at: http://www.realfastbook.com/

ABOUT THE AUTHOR

Daniel Hall is a bestselling author, speaker, publisher, nurse, attorney, and host of the Real Fast Results Podcast at www.RealFastResults.com. He is also the creator of the highly popular Real Fast™ brand of training products. And host of the top-ranked business podcast. He left law practice 10 years ago to build his publishing business and has never looked back. Daniel is a true serial entrepreneur, and his list of URLs is longer than a piece of paper. You can check out Daniel's hub at www. DanielHallPresents.com.

Daniel's first product was the super-successful and very popular Speak on Cruise Ships program, which is designed to help speakers trade their public-speaking talents on lux-ury cruise ships worldwide (See *http://amzn.to/1VQRpwS*).

FREE 7-DAY VIDEO COURSE

Step-by-Step Training Shows You How to Publish Your
Very Own Print-on-Demand Book on Amazon

Open browser and navigate to
http://RealFastBook.com/

Have You Subscribed to
The Real Fast Results Podcast Yet?
Subscribe Here: *http://realfastresults.com/itunes*

Why?
Because each show is like a high-quality info-product
that delivers the exact steps you need to get the results we
promise in the title of the episode!

It's like a premium subscription to a high-caliber marketing membership site—FOR FREE!

All you have to do is subscribe and listen here—
http://realfastresults.com/itunes

INTERESTED IN PUBLISHING & SELLING YOUR WRITING?

Check Out Daniel's "Real Fast"™ Training
Programs . . .

Real Fast Book
http://realfastbook.com/

Real Fast Audio Book
http://realfastaudiobook.com/

Real Fast Library Marketing
http://realfastlibrarymarketing.com/

Real Fast Book Marketing
http://realfastbookmarketing.com

Real Fast Public Domain
http://realfastpublicdomain.com

Real Fast Info Product
http://realfastinfoproduct.com/

Real Fast Derivative Product
http://realfastderivativeproducts.com/

Real Fast Email Marketing
http://realfastemailmarketing.com/

Real Fast TV PR
http://realfasttvpr.com/

Real Fast iProducts
http://realfastiproducts.com/

Read Fast Indie Book Marketing
http:// realfastindiebookmarketing.com

REAL FAST NOTES

REAL FAST NOTES

REAL FAST NOTES

REAL FAST NOTES

REAL FAST NOTES

REAL FAST NOTES

REAL FAST NOTES

REAL FAST NOTES

REAL FAST NOTES

REAL FAST NOTES

REAL FAST NOTES

REAL FAST NOTES

REAL FAST NOTES

63309910R00077

Made in the USA
Lexington, KY
03 May 2017